Crayola

Ultimate Sticker and Activity Book

BuzzPop

Hello!
Connect the dots to see who is waving to you.

Answers on page 61

Colorful Rows
Crayons come in so many colors.
Find the sticker for the one that comes
next in each row.

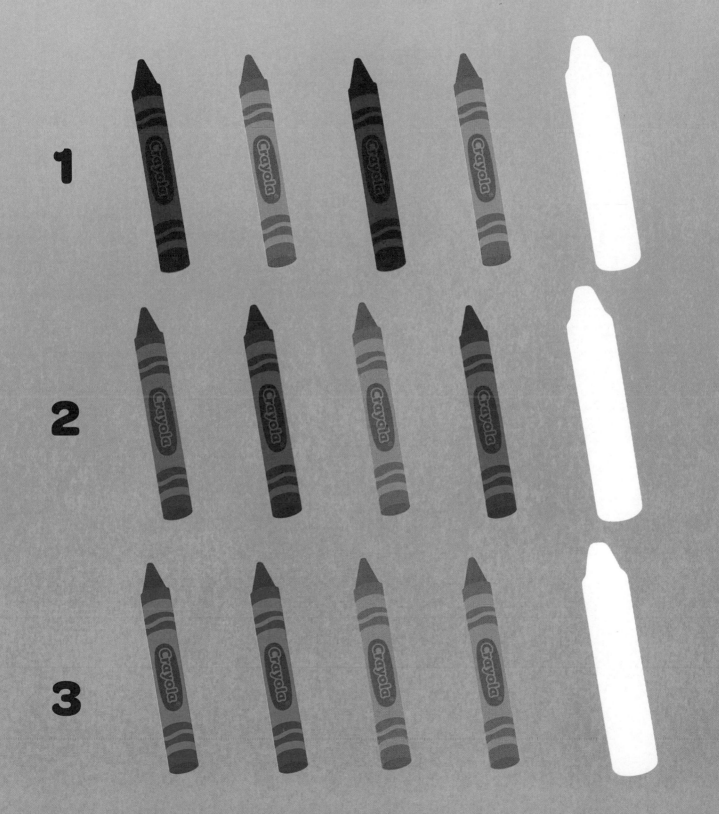

Magical Changes

This fairy can magically change her appearance.
Can you circle the 5 differences between the images?

Royal Fashion

A yellow dress with silver sparkles, please!

Feeling Fancy
What does a princess wear in the summertime?
Circle the objects to make your princess the best dressed!

Name That Animal!
Draw a line to match each animal to its name.

Turtle

Lion

Bat

What's Hatching?
How many eggs are in the nest?

Your answer:

Answers on page 61

9

Welcome to the Farm
The farm is a busy place.
Put farm stickers in this space.

Farm Friends
Put a circle around each farm animal that is brown.
How many did you find?

Your answer:

Answers on page 61

Who Says "Cock-a-Doodle-Doo"?
Connect the dots to find out. Then color the picture.

Back to the Barn

The cow had a nice day out in the field. Now it's time to go back to the barn. Help her get there.

Answers on page 62

Fantasy Under the Sea

Can you decorate this castle for a seashell fairy?
Color it in and add some stickers!

The Amazing Ocean

Use your stickers to show all the
creatures who live in the sea!

A Colorful Fish
Use the guide to finish the picture.

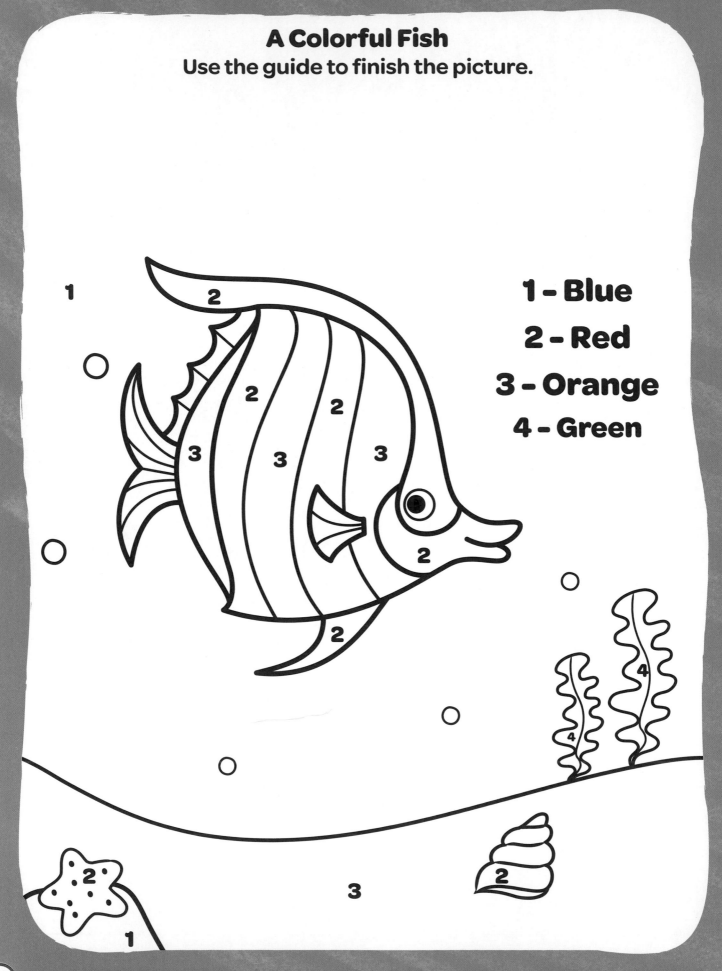

1 - Blue
2 - Red
3 - Orange
4 - Green

Fin to Fin
Which path will get the fish to his friend?

Your answer:

Swimming in the Sea

Draw a line to match each animal that lives in the ocean to its name.

Seahorse

Crab

Fish

Answers on page 62

Underwater Adventure
Draw some interesting sea creatures for this scuba diver to discover.

Blue Bubbles
How many bubbles are there?

Your answer:

Answers on page 62

Ahoy, Mateys!
Use your stickers to complete the picture of this fishy pirate!

Here in the Jungle

Trees and grass make a jungle green.
Jungle animals will complete the scene.
Add your jungle animal stickers here!

I Spy Butterflies!
Follow the flowers to get this zebra to the butterflies.

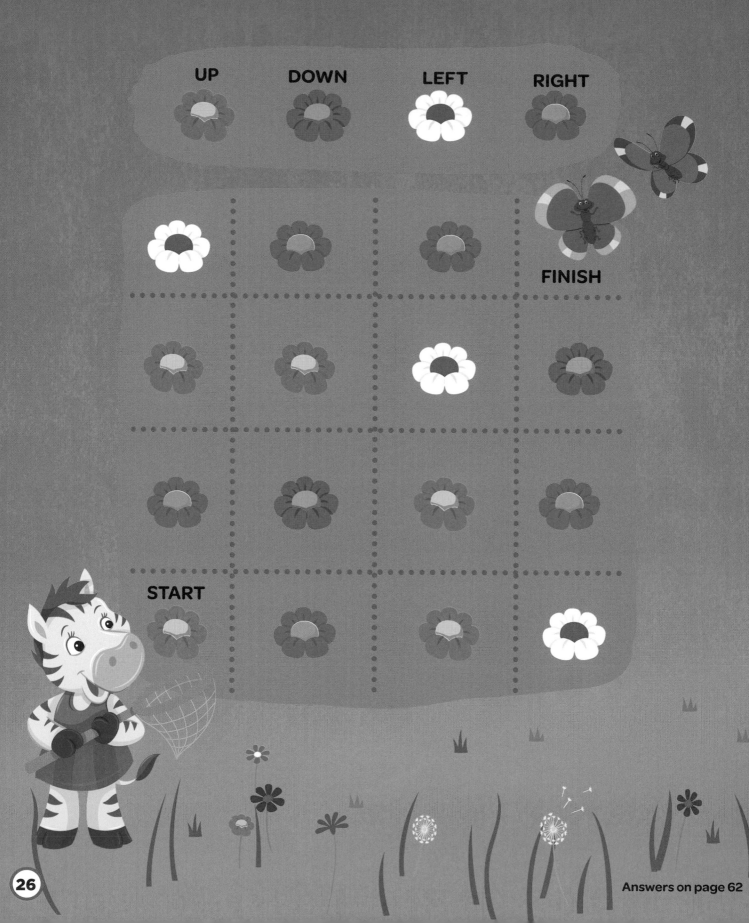

UP   DOWN   LEFT   RIGHT

FINISH

START

Answers on page 62

Three Jungle Critters

Each of these animals should appear once in each row and column. Use stickers to fill the empty squares.

Weight Lifting Champ

No one can lift more weight than this gorilla can!
Give him a trophy sticker for his strength.
Draw some bananas for him, too.

Look at Me!

Most parrots have very bright colors. Color this one in as many bright colors as you can.

It's a Jungle in Here
Find and circle these animals' names in the puzzle below.

HIPPO   SNAKE   ZEBRA   RHINO

H W J O M P O
Q I W L O I Z
L S P Q N Z E
V I F P I U B
L X Y L O Q R
V S N A K E A
I R H I N O G

What's for Lunch?
In the thought balloon above his head,
draw what the elephant is thinking
of eating for lunch.

Design a Zebra
Most zebras have stripes. But this one can have any pattern and be any colors you like!

Hanging Around

What colors do you think this snake curled up
on this branch should be? You decide!

Bike Riders

Get the hedgehog bike rider to his friend so they can ride together!

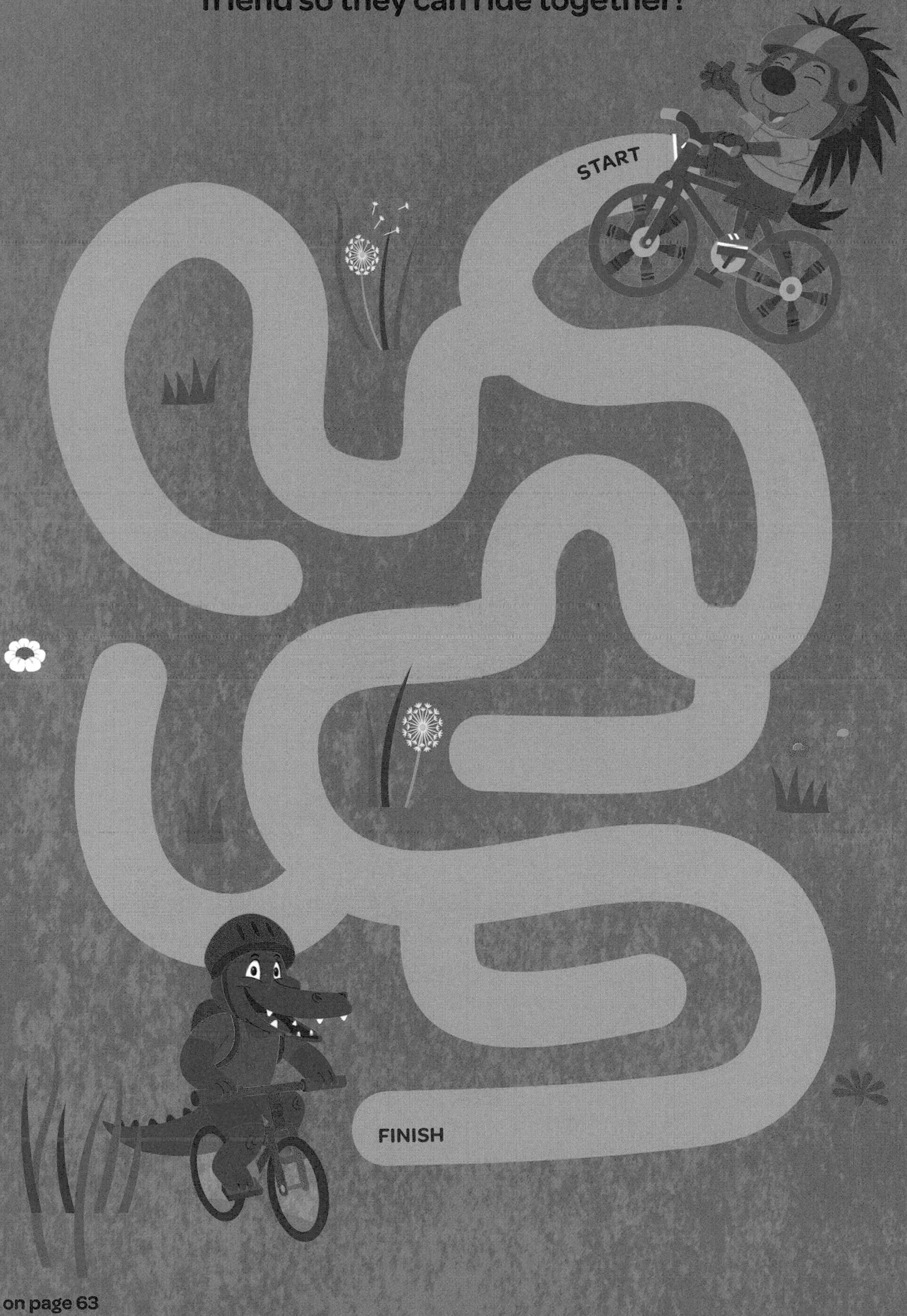

START

FINISH

Out in the Yard
Fill in this scene with your backyard animal stickers!

Backyard Visitors

Find and circle the names of these animals
that might be in your backyard.

CAT   BIRD   BEE   SKUNK   SNAIL

```
Y  T  U  I  S  B
C  A  T  Z  K  E
B  I  R  D  U  E
M  I  S  P  N  U
X  O  Y  L  K  Q
S  N  A  I  L  P
```

Answers on page 63

Go Fetch!
Get this dog to his ball!

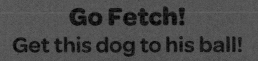

START

FINISH

Squeak, Squeak . . .
Find and circle the mouse that is different from the others.

Answers on page 63

Garden Playground

A backyard garden is a great place to play!
Color in this fun scene!

Ribbit, Ribbit!

Copy this friendly frog's smiling face into the
empty grid on the next page, square by square.
Then color both froggy faces.

In the Forest
A forest has a lot of trees.
Add some stickers as you please!

We Love Camping!

Color this cozy camp scene and add some buggy stickers.

Count the Candles!
How many candles are on the cake?
Count them up and write the number.
Remember to make a wish!

Your answer:

Rabbits Love Carrots

Can you circle the 5 differences between these two scenes?

Who Says "Meow"?

Connect the dots and see! Then color the picture.

My Favorite Animal

Draw a picture of your favorite animal in the picture frame.

Fluttering Butterflies

Find the two butterflies that are the same and color them.
Then color all the other butterflies different colors!
How many butterflies are there in all?

Your answer: _____

Answers on page 64

Count the Bees, Please
How many bees do you see buzzing around?

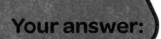

Your answer:

Pretty Birdie
Use the guide to finish the picture.

1 - Blue
2 - Orange
3 - Brown
4 - Green

In His Paws

What is the puppy holding in his paws?
Write down the first letter and then every
second letter in the circle to find out.

START HERE

S L G T N L E P O L C P W A I S B S

_____ _____ _____ _____ _____ _____ _____ _____

Which Way to Earth?
Which path will get this space traveler to planet Earth?

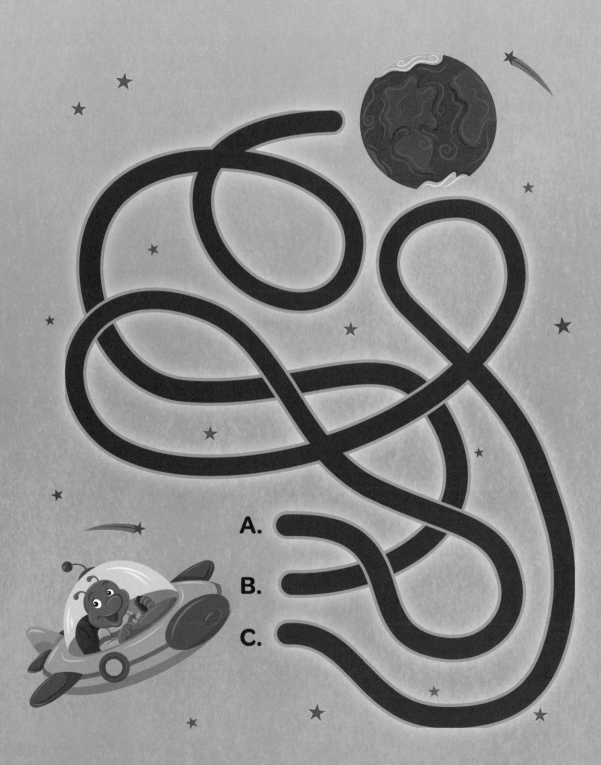

A.

B.

C.

Answers on page 64

Out-of-This-World Mail!

Pretend you are an astronaut and write a postcard to your best friend on Earth. Describe what you are seeing. Then, add a sticker stamp.

PLACE STAMP HERE

Now You Know the Wonderful World
Give yourself a reward sticker in the spaces
below next to each scene you've completed

Farm

Yard

Ocean

Forest

Jungle

VACATION TIME

Answers

Page 2

Page 3

1   2   3

Pages 4–5

Page 7

Page 8

Turtle

Lion

Bat

Page 9

4 eggs

Page 12

Page 13

Page 14

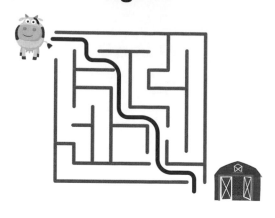

Page 19

Page 20

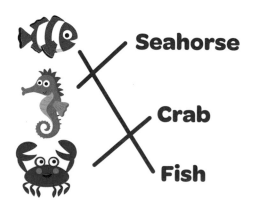

Seahorse

Crab

Fish

Page 22

There are 7 bubbles

Page 23

Page 26

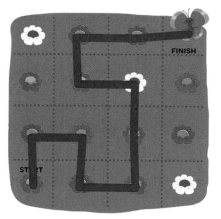

Page 27

Page 31

Page 35

Page 38

Page 39

Page 40

Page 47

There are 5 candles

Pages 48-49

Page 50

Page 52
There are 5 butterflies

Page 53
There are 4 bees

Page 55
SNOWBALL

Page 56

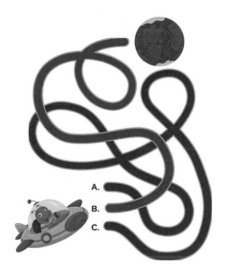

Page 3

Page 23

Page 27

Page 36

Page 44

Page 58